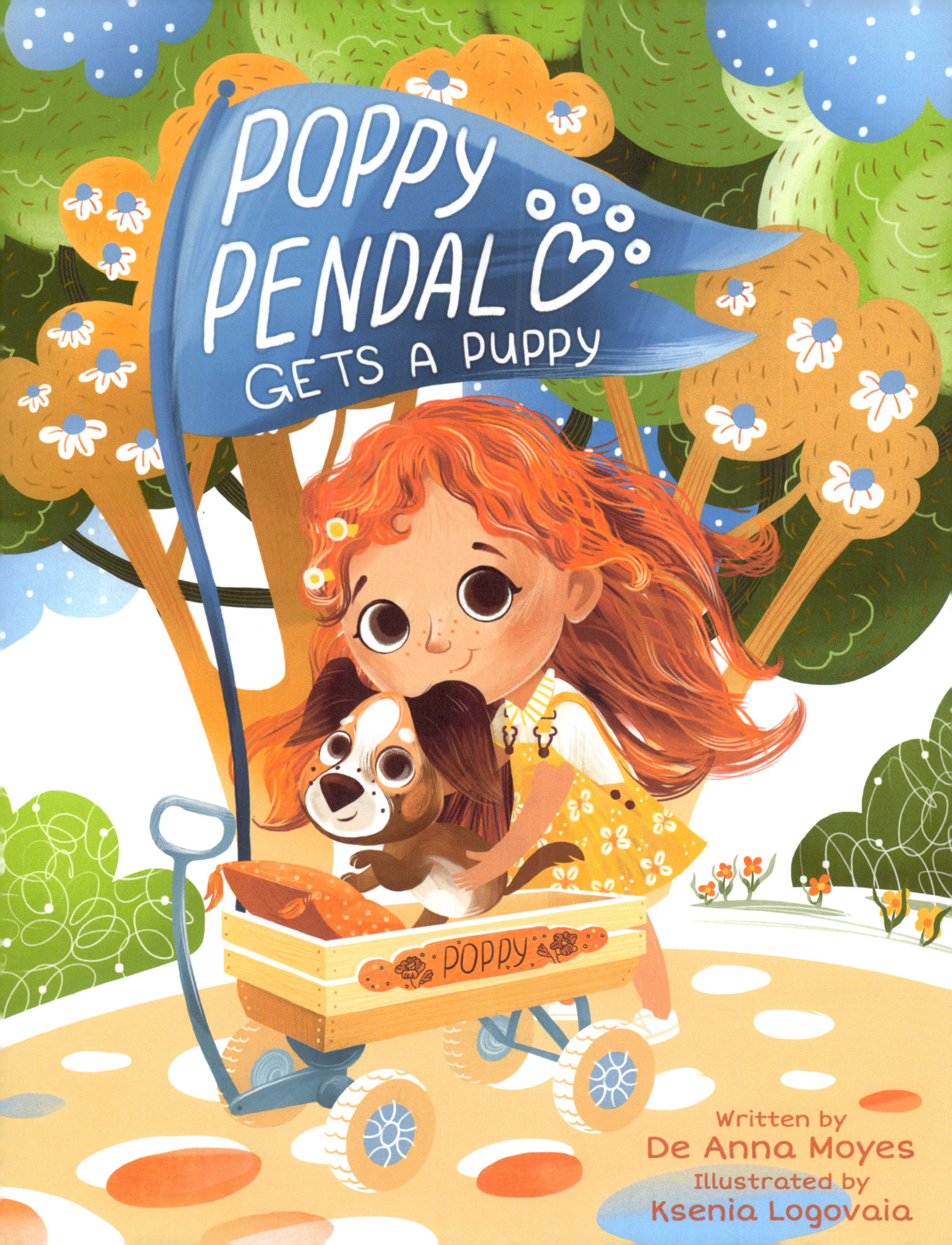

Poppy Pendal Gets a Puppy
Copyright © 2023 by De Anna Moyes
Illustrations by Ksenia Logovaia

All rights reserved. No part of this publication may be reproduced, distributed, or transmitted in any form or by any means, including photocopying, recording or other electronic or mechanical methods, without the prior written permission of the author, except in the case of brief quotations embodied in reviews and certain other non-commercial uses permitted by copyright law.

Printed in the United States of America

Hardcover ISBN: 978-1-961624-02-3
Paperback ISBN: 978-1-961624-03-0
Ebook ISBN: 978-1-961624-04-7
Library of Congress Control Number: 2023943315

DartFrog Kids
A division of DartFrog Books
PO Box 867
Manchester, VT 05254
Dartfrogbooks.com

I dedicate this book to the
LGBTQ+ community and to my
loving, supportive family.
Thank you for always believing in me
and for being such great cheerleaders.
Love to all.

Poppy skipped out of the grocery store,
munching on an ice cream bar.

"Mommy," she said.
"When we get home, can we—"

Poppy stopped in her tracks,
as her eyes landed
on the most wonderful thing
she had ever seen.

"Puppies!" Poppy shrieked, racing over to greet the playpen of wiggling furballs.

The lady from the local pet adoption center laughed. "Would you like to hold one?"

Poppy nodded, her hair bobbing furiously. "Yes, please! I'd love to!"

Poppy was just bending down to pick up a puppy when she felt someone squeeze in next to her. Two hands reached into the box and scooped up the very puppy she had been reaching for.

"Hey, puppy, I'm back!" a young boy said to the puppy. Then to the lady, he said, "Thank you for letting us adopt him. We'll take very good care of him."

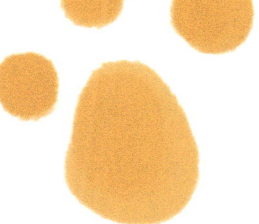

Poppy watched longingly as the
boy ran off with the puppy.

Tugging on her mother's arm, Poppy
said, "Mommy, please can we adopt a
puppy, too? We can give it a good home.
I promise to help take care of it!"

Her mother smiled. "Yes, Poppy. We've
already been approved for adoption.
We knew they would be here today.
We just wanted to surprise you!"

"Yay!" Poppy cheered.

Leaning in, Poppy picked up a sleeping puppy. To her surprise, he only had three legs!

Suddenly, the puppy let out a big yawn. Then, opening its eyes, it licked Poppy right on the cheek.

Poppy giggled as he wagged his tail happily. "You're so cute! But what happened to your leg?"

"He was just born that way," the lady told Poppy. "It happens sometimes. He'll still make a fine pet."

Poppy grinned and gave the puppy a loving squeeze. "He's more than fine. He's perfect!"

At home, Poppy set her new puppy down in the front yard.

"Welcome to your new home . . ." Poppy started. Then she stopped, confused. "Mommy, what should we call him? I forgot to ask if he had a name."

"How about Spot?"

Poppy thought about it. "No, he doesn't seem like a Spot to me. Well, I guess I'll think of something!"

Poppy walked up the porch stairs but stopped half-way. Behind her, the puppy struggled up one slow step at a time. She waited patiently for him to catch up.

Poppy and her mommies did everything
they could to make it easier for
her new puppy to get around.

Her mommies built a ramp
for the back steps.

Poppy made him a cozy bed
with a blanket to rest in.

And when he got tired, Poppy pulled him in her wagon or carried him in a pouch.

Soon, Poppy and her new puppy were inseparable.

They watched television together.

They ate their meals at the same time.
(Peanut butter cookies were
their favorite dessert!)

They played hopscotch.

They swam in her small swimming pool.

They colored before bedtime.

They even cuddled together before falling asleep.

There was just one problem:
Poppy still hadn't found a name
that suited the little guy.

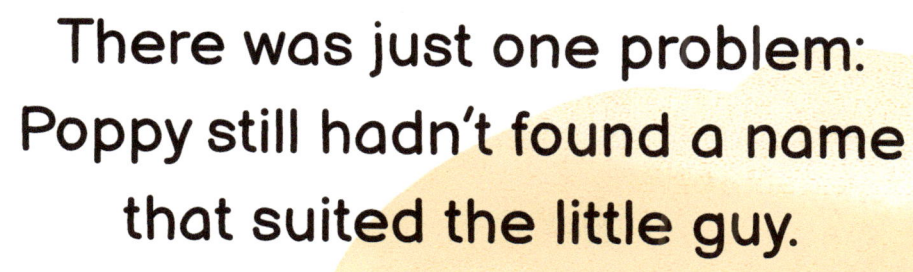

Poppy and her puppy had been together for a few weeks when Poppy took him to meet her grandparents.

"Well, what do we have here?" asked Grandpa Hamish.

"He's my new puppy!" beamed Poppy.

Grandma Tilly smiled.
"A new puppy? What's his name?"

Poppy frowned. "I'm still waiting to find the right one," she said at last.

"How about Buddy?" her grandfather asked.

"Buddy?" Poppy repeated. "No, he doesn't seem like a Buddy to me."

"What about Toby?" Grandma Tilly asked.

"Toby?" Poppy repeated. "No, he doesn't seem like a Toby to me, either."

"Well, I'm sure you'll find the right name soon enough," Grandpa Hamish said. "Come on. Let's go play in the backyard."

Together, the three of them played hide-and-seek. Poppy was able to easily dodge her grandpa, but the puppy had a hard time keeping up.

"Poppy," her grandfather called. "Bring that little pup of yours into my workshop. I've got just the thing for him."

Poppy loved her grandfather's workshop. He was always creating something new and exciting in there. She wondered what he might have for her puppy.

"Here we go!" Grandpa Hamish said, holding up a small wheel.
"This ought to do the trick!"

Poppy watched in wonder as her grandpa made a little harness out of a brown leather strap and attached it to the wheel. When he was done, he looped the harness around the puppy and set him on the grass.

"There you go, little fella! This is going to make it much easier for you to get around!"

Poppy and her grandfather cheered as her puppy raced around them with his new leg.

"Look at him go, Grandpa!" Poppy squealed with delight. "He loves his new wheel!"

Poppy giggled as the puppy weaved between their legs.

"That's it! I just thought of the perfect name for him," smiled Poppy. "I'm going to call him Wheelson."

"I think that name suits him very well," her grandpa chuckled.

"It's perfect!" said Poppy. "Just like him."

About the Author

De Anna Moyes is from Los Angeles, California. She is happily married with four children, and a pup that keeps them on their toes. She wrote her first children's book in elementary school which won first place and was on display at the county fair.

When she is not writing at home, De Anna spends most of her time traveling the world and looking for her next big adventure. She is always on the lookout for a great cup of coffee! You can easily find her at an outdoor café enjoying a latte and smiling at everyone who passes her by.

De Anna is someone who sees the beauty in the world and in the uniqueness in others. Through her children's books, she hopes to spread love, joy, kindness, and acceptance with the stories she tells.

De Anna also writes chapter books and Women's Fiction. Be sure to follow her on Instagram @deannamoyes or at https://deannawritesbooks.com, to learn when Poppy and Wheelson go on their next adventure!

About the Illustrator

Ksenia Logovaia is a Belarusian artist and illustrator, a mom and traveller, a dog and horse lover! She comes from Minsk, Belarus and now lives in Poland. She adores drawing and painting while traveling—her sketchbook is always with her. She illustrated The Feather Necklace during a cold, Nordic winter, taking in the spirit of tropical heat and colors.

Printed in the USA
CPSIA information can be obtained
at www.ICGtesting.com
LVHW071228201023
761064LV00019B/27